Fashion Subscription Box

A Step-by-Step Guide to Launching a Curated Style Business

Table of Contents

Chapter 1. Introduction

Step right into the vibrant world of fashion with our special report, "Fashion Subscription Box: A Step-by-Step Guide to Launching a Curated Style Business." Whether you're a fashion enthusiast, up-and-coming stylist, or aspiring entrepreneur, you'll find exactly what you need to get your foot in the door of this lucrative and trend-setting industry. Bursting with insider advice and strategic tips, this comprehensive guide serves as your blueprint to not just launching, but also nurturing and scaling your unique spin on the fashion subscription box business. Get ready to turn passion into profit, style into substance, and little details into big success with this must-have guide. So why wait? Grab this special report and take the exciting first steps toward making your fashion-forward dreams come true!

Chapter 2. Understanding the Market: The Rise of Fashion Subscription Boxes

Subscription boxes have seen a significant boom in popularity over the last decade. The concept of receiving a curated box of products delivered directly to your door, tailored to your tastes and needs, has become a staple of modern consumer behavior. Nowhere is this trend more prevalent than in the world of fashion.

2.1. The Emergence of Subscription Boxes

The subscription box model originated from the magazine and newspaper industry but transitioned to physical goods with the rise of the internet. The first pioneers were companies like Dollar Shave Club and Birchbox, pushing everyday essentials.

The appeal lies in the excitement of opening a new box of unknown goodies each month—an amalgamation of Christmas morning and personal shopping experience. The enthusiasm for subscription boxes has since expanded into the fashion industry, where personal tastes, the desire for novelty, and the draw of convenience have fueled the rise of fashion subscription boxes.

2.2. Fashion Subscription Box: A New Frontier for the Industry

The fashion industry has always been at the forefront of change and innovation, swiftly adapting to new technologies and shifting consumer behaviors. The emergence of e-commerce radically altered how consumers interact with fashion, allowing for unprecedented global reach, deeper customer relationships, and direct-to-consumer models.

Fashion subscription boxes present another window of opportunity. They not only deliver style and convenience but also provide a personalized experience that is so cherished by the modern consumer. Subscription services like Stitch Fix, Nordstrom's Trunk Club, and Rent the Runway have disrupted the traditional retail models, capitalizing on data-driven personalization and the surprise and delight factor of unboxing.

2.3. Understanding the Market: Who Subscribes and Why

To be successful in the fashion subscription box industry, it is crucial to understand your customer. Research has shown that the typical subscriber is a 30-44 year old, affluent woman living in an urban setting. Nonetheless, there are numerous 'micro-markets' within this demographic pool, such as eco-conscious consumers looking for sustainable fashion, plus-sized women seeking more diverse style options, or busy professionals needing workwear solutions.

The motivations for subscribing to fashion boxes are varied and manifold. Convenience and personalization top the list, with customers loving the customized styles delivered to their doorsteps, saving them time and mitigating decision fatigue. The thrill of discovery and the appeal of stepping out of their comfort zone with expert selected trends also play essential roles.

2.4. Competition and Differentiation

Despite the proliferation of fashion subscription boxes, the market is incredibly competitive. Success in this industry requires distinction.

Your unique selling proposition (USP) could lie in niche market targeting, product or brand partnerships, superior personalization algorithms, or sustainability efforts. Also, practice such as sourcing from local artisans or using eco-friendly packaging can greatly appeal to specific audiences.

2.5. Market Trends and Future Prospects

The global fashion subscription market is expected to grow at an incredible rate in the coming years. This potential is primarily seen in developing economies like Asia, where e-commerce and digital consumption are skyrocketing. However, Western markets continue to hold strong potential, as consumers continually adapt to virtual shopping experiences.

Moreover, as AI and machine learning become increasingly sophisticated, they offer opportunities for enhanced personalization and improved style predictions—further driving customer satisfaction and retention.

2.6. Conclusion

Understanding the market is the first vital step in launching a successful fashion subscription box business. The key is to blend the traditional allure of personal shopping with modern technology's benefits, tailoring each box to the individual subscriber while balancing variety and consistency. As the fashion industry continues to evolve, so does the innovative model of fashion subscription boxes, opening up endless opportunities for those prepared to seize them.

Chapter 3. Designing Your Business Plan: From Concept to Blueprint

Launching a carefully-thought-out fashion subscription box service requires more than just knowledge of the latest trends – you also need an efficient business plan as your roadmap to success. Mapping numerous vital aspects, such as understanding your target market to financial forecasting, your business plan is a concrete document that provides you with the entire landscape of your enterprise.

3.1. Identifying Your Target Market

Your fashion subscription box can't be everything to everyone. Make sure you know who your service is for. Identifying your target market is a strategic move that impacts every other aspect of your business plan. Identify the age group, gender, and geographic location of your ideal customer. Are you targeting stylish millennials or fashion-conscious working women? Clearly defined demographics lead to effective marketing strategies.

Don't just stop at demographics. Delve into their problems, aspirations, and hobbies. What problems can your subscription box solve for them? What value will it add to their lives? Crafting detailed customer personas will aid you in understanding who you are serving and how to serve them better.

3.2. Assessing the Competition

To carve out a successful niche for your subscription service, you must understand what's already out there. Conduct a SWOT (Strengths, Weaknesses, Opportunities, Threats) analysis of your competition. See what they're doing right, what they're doing wrong, and how you can do things differently to stand out.

However, remember to include not just direct competitors (other subscription box services), but also indirect competitors — places where your target audience currently shops for fashion items.

3.3. Determining Your Unique Selling Proposition (USP)

What makes your subscription box different? Is it hand-curated? Are the items rare, sustainable, or created by emerging designers? Your USP is the key factor that sets you apart from the competition. It is the compelling argument that prompts a consumer to choose your service over another.

To clarify your USP, aim to fulfill an existing gap in the market. Perhaps there's a lack of affordable luxury items or an absence of subscription boxes dedicated to plus-size fashion. Look at what your target market wants but is not getting and step in to fill that need.

3.4. Crafting Your Brand Narrative

Your brand is more than just a name or logo - it is the story you tell your customers about who you are, what you practice, and what you promise. It speaks to your values, your personality, and the benefits you offer.

Remember, people engage with stories and brands that spark emotion. Your narrative could revolve around empowering consumers, supporting indie artists, advocating sustainability, or simply sparking joy with surprise fashion items.

3.5. Planning Your Marketing Strategy

Once you have understood your customer, competition, USP, and brand narrative, you need to plan how you will bring your product to your audience.

This could span various channels like social media advertising, strategic collaborations with influencers, SEO driven blog posts, or targeted email marketing. Whatever you choose, ensure that it is based on robust data on where your customers are most likely to see you and react positively.

3.6. Financial Planning

Deciding how to price your subscription boxes can make or break your business. You want to cover your costs and make a profit, while also ensuring the price point is attractive to your potential customers.

Your costs will include procuring the fashion items, packaging, shipping, and return, as well as any marketing expenditures. You should also factor in some scope for unpredictable costs. Aim to have a profit margin that facilitates growth while keeping prices reasonable for consumers.

In addition, you should also map out a detailed financial projection including cash-flow, breakeven analysis, and capital requirements for the days to come.

3.7. Operations and Logistics

Now, turn your attention to the practical aspects of running a subscription box service. How and where will you source items? How will you package your boxes so that they're visually appealing when they arrive, yet not too costly or wasteful? How will you handle shipping, both domestically and internationally, and how will you manage returns?

Consider making a list of potential suppliers, calculating the cost and time of packaging, and researching various courier services and their policies.

Remember, the satisfaction of your subscriber frequently pivots on the timely delivery and unboxing experience.

3.8. Establishing Key Metrics

Finally, you'll want to establish some key metrics to guide your path as you grow. These could include churn rate, customer acquisition cost, customer lifetime value, and average revenue per user.

Constantly measure and analyze these metrics as they will provide invaluable information on where to invest more and which areas need improvement.

In wrapping, your business plan reveals the smart mechanics and heart moving elements that will combine to make your fashion subscription box not just a business, but a beloved brand. With each step, keep patience and remain consistent. All the best, and may the fashion be with you!

Chapter 4. Finding Your Niche: Identifying Your Style and Target Audience

In the crowded realm of fashion, carving out a niche means identifying your unique style and aligning it with an equally unique audience. How do you do this? What questions should you ask and what factors should you consider? We'll walk you through the entire process from introspection to market research to strategic execution.

4.1. Understanding Your Unique Style

Every fashion enthusiast has a style of their own- a distinct yet ever-evolving fashion fingerprint, if you will. The first step to finding your niche in the fashion subscription boxes industry is to understand your unique style. What are your personal fashion tastes and preferences? How would you describe your style aesthetic in a few key words? Casual Chic? Vintage Glam? Boho Refined? Luxurious Minimalism? There's no right or wrong answer.

Next, consider how your style fits into the larger context of fashion. Is it tied to specific designers, fashion movements, eras or cultures? Does it lean towards certain materials, patterns or cuts?

Finally, think about what makes your style unique. Maybe it's your ability to blend unlikely pieces together or your flair for finding the perfect accessories. Or perhaps it's your knack for using fashion as a form of self-expression that can echo an individual's personality, interests and lifestyle.

Document your answers and observations. This 'Style Profile' isn't a rigid definition of your fashion identity, but rather a launching pad for deeper understanding and inspiration.

4.2. Identifying Your Target Audience

After defining your unique style, the next step is to identify who your target audience is. Remember, not everyone will be interested in what you have to offer and that's okay. In fact, targeting a specific audience makes marketing easier and increases the chances of customer satisfaction.

Begin by asking a simple question- who would appreciate and align with your style? Consider demographics such as age range, gender, location, income level and occupation. Just remember that these are basic guidelines, not restrictions. You should have as broad a view of your potential audience as possible without losing sight of your niche.

Beyond demographics, mull over the psychographics- the attitudes, aspirations, interests, lifestyles and other non-quantitative aspects of your target audience. Where do they shop? What magazines or blogs do they read? What social media platforms do they use? What types of events do they attend? What charities do they support?

4.3. Building A Customer Persona

A great way to better understand your target audience is by creating customer personas. These are detailed profiles of fictional individuals who represent the different segments of your audience.

Start by giving your persona a name, an age, and a profession. Then, delve deeper. How would they describe their style? What are their shopping habits? What social media platforms do they frequent? What challenges do they face when shopping for clothes? The more detailed you can make your personas, the better you'll understand your audience.

4.4. Intersecting Your Style With Your Audience

Now that you've identified your unique style and potential audience, it's time to find out where they intersect. Consider how you can adapt and mold your style to your audience's tastes and preferences.

Are there certain pieces that resonate with them more? Do they gravitate towards certain fabrics, colors or patterns? Are they more interested in classic, timeless pieces or trendy, seasonal picks? Additionally, understand their needs and criteria- convenience, comfort, uniqueness, sustainability and so on.

You can find this information in a few ways. Social media is a goldmine- look at accounts they follow, posts they like, and reviews they've given. Online surveys and interviews too can provide valuable insights. Don't forget to keep an eye on competitors who are targeting the same audience.

4.5. Testing Your Idea

Before diving headfirst into launching your business, validate your idea. Test your box concept with a small group from your target audience. Consider factors such as the price points, the frequency of the subscription, the packaging, the number of items in each box — anything that will be part of their subscription experience.

Incorporate their feedback to refine your business model. If a piece isn't a hit, swap it for something else. If a box feels too sparse or too crowded, adjust the quantity. Measure satisfaction levels and always aim to exceed expectations.

4.6. Staying Relevant

Remember, fashion is constantly evolving, and so should your subscription box business. Stay on top of latest trends, emerging designers and changing consumer attitudes. Consistently revisit and revise your style and audience to ensure your business is always fresh, relevant and thriving.

In conclusion, finding your niche requires introspection, research and lots of testing. It may seem daunting at first, but once you've found your sweet spot, your fashion box will be a fantastic fusion of your unique style and your audience's tastes and needs.

Chapter 5. Sourcing Your Products: Building Relationships with Suppliers

Experience shows that being serious about sourcing your products right from the beginning can have a massive effect on the success of your business. It's about creating a comfortable, consistent experience for your customers - one that also feels personalized. Therefore, choosing good quality, suitable pieces for your box, and building a solid relationship with your suppliers, forms the backbone of your fashion subscription box journey.

5.1. Understanding What You Need

Before you start seeking suppliers, you need to have a clear idea of the product range you want to offer. Here, your customer research plays a critical role. Identify the age group, style preferences, typical income and common needs of your target audience. This information will form the framework for your product sourcing strategy.

Also, decide on the specific items you want to include in your box. Are you aiming for a general mix of apparel and accessories, or do you have a niche focus? Will these items vary between boxes, or will your box have a standard template?

Your clarified needs are the roadmap to finding the right suppliers. They will guide you to know what to look for and assist in having clear discussions with potential suppliers.

5.2. Researching Prospective Suppliers

Once you have outlined what you need, it's time to identify potential suppliers. This step often involves diligent research as new suppliers are sprouting up every day, each offering something slightly different than the rest.

There are several ways to go about researching suppliers:

1. Online searches: One of the easiest and most common methods is to simply search for wholesale suppliers of the goods you're interested in.

2. Trade shows and exhibitions: These provide an opportunity to meet suppliers face-to-face and examine their products first-hand.

3. Industry directories: These can be a valuable reference for finding reputable suppliers.

4. Networking: Connect with other business owners in the industry for supplier recommendations.

Remember, you are hunting for a business partner rather than a simple service. Therefore, assess the supplier's commitment to quality, speed of delivery, pricing, and communication skills.

5.3. Making Contact with Prospective Suppliers

After identifying potential suppliers, making contact is your next step. An introduction via email or a phone call can do wonders. Lay out your plans and requirements clearly. State your business goals, your intended customer base and inquire as to whether their products, price range, and supply chain could accommodate your needs.

Remember, good suppliers get approached by many resellers. So, it's essential to be professional in your approach and make your potential value apparent.

5.4. Evaluating Your Suppliers

If several suppliers meet your needs on paper, your next step should be to evaluate them. This entails a variety of tasks:

1. Collating their quotes: This will allow you to compare their pricing.

2. Assessing the quality: Either order samples, or if physically possible, visit the supplier to examine goods first-hand and assess their quality.

3. Checking references: Ask the suppliers to provide contact details of some of their clients, particularly ones in the same line of business as you.

As you grow, your credibility and influence with your supplier will grow too. As such, it always helps to have open lines of communication and a positive relationship.

5.5. Negotiating Terms

Your relationship with your supplier isn't necessarily just a buyer-seller one. There are many details you can negotiate to make the terms more favorable for you:

1. Contract length: Suppliers are more willing to give better deals for longer-term contracts.

2. Payment terms: Negotiating payment terms can help manage your cash flow.

Remember, the best business relationships are win-win. So, while you want terms to be as favorable for you as possible, they should benefit your suppliers too.

5.6. Forming and Cementing Relationships

If you're happy with the suppliers you've found, it's time to start forming a relationship. Regular communication goes a long way here. Talk frequently with your suppliers, keep them updated about your plans, and keep your feedback about their products detailed and constructive.

A strong relationship with your supplier also means there's likely to be more room for negotiation, better support when issues arise, and the possibility of more favorable terms as your business grows.

In a nutshell, building relationships with suppliers is vital for a successful subscription box business. It takes effort and dedication, not just to find a suitable supplier, but to maintain a prosperous and productive relationship. Consider suppliers as partners in your journey, and your fashion-forward dreams will be well on their way to becoming a stylish, profitable reality.

Chapter 6. Creative Curation: The Art and Science of Box Design

To create a successful fashion subscription box business, the key lies within an artful blend of curation and engaging design. Your business proposition will not merely be about selling clothing articles, but about delivering an experience.

6.1. From Concept to Curation

Curating a fashion subscription box begins at the ideation stage. Your concept's clarity sets the course for the subsequent stages, so define your target market first. Consider the demographic and psychographic aspects. Who is your ideal customer? What do they want from a fashion subscription box? Understanding these facets of your customer's profile will guide your curation steps.

Once you've established your audience, decide on a core style. This might be trendy, vintage, timeless, or even adapted to a certain lifestyle or profession. Establishing a distinct style for your box will help position it in a niche, trimming down the competition.

6.2. Box Elements

Your fashion subscription box will consist of multiple items. These can include clothes, accessories, footwear, and other complementary products like fashion magazines or beauty items. It's crucial that you carefully select every item. They should add value to the box and resonate with your target audience's expectations.

Achieving a balance within your box elements is crucial. There's beauty in harmony, so the piecing together of different but complementary items should tell a story or follow a theme. This balance can be based on a seasonal trend, a palette, a niche style, or different aspects of fashion.

To ensure a satisfying unboxing experience, consider including detailed style cards, which not only let customers know the details of the garments and accessories they've received but can also provide styling tips, suggested outfits, and the story behind your curated items.

6.3. The Science of Designing the Box

You want your subscription box to make a statement, and the design of your box is the initial communication the customers will have with your brand. Hence, it necessitates thoughtful planning.

Begin by considering your box size. It needs to be large enough to hold your fashion items without crumpling or damaging them, but also not so big that items move around excessively. Balance practicality with presentation.

Next, attend to the outer appearance of your box. The graphic design should resonate with your brand vibe and act as a teaser of what's inside. Choose colors, logos, and typography that align with your brand identity.

Similarly, the interior of the box is part of the unboxing experience. A well-designed, personalized interior enhances the customer's curiosity and enjoyment. Adding messages or quotes can provide an interactive and delightful touch.

6.4. Ephemeral Touchpoints in Design

Equally crucial are the ephemeral touchpoints of your design - the transient but impactful elements that your customers will remember. The openability of your box, the arrangement of the items, the scent that wafts out when it's opened, as well as the tactile feel of the box matters. Each of these elements should be curated to elicit anticipation, pleasure, and satisfaction.

6.5. Eco-friendly Packaging

Eco-friendly packaging is not just a selling point but a corporate responsibility. Consider using recyclable materials for your boxes and insulation. Opting for low-impact materials, such as recycled paper or biodegradable plastics, signals responsibility and will be appreciated by environmentally conscious customers.

6.6. The Complete Experience

The customer experience doesn't end at the unboxing. You're creating a community and a relationship. Survey your customers, and use their feedback for future curation. Send follow-up emails featuring the upcoming month's theme or offering styling tips. Engage on social media with comments, shares, and reposts. This active involvement completes the curation process, turning one-off purchasers into loyal customers.

In conclusion, creative curation is a meticulous process combining both art and science. It's about understanding your customer, presenting a cohesive aesthetic, and enhancing their overall experience. A fabulously curated fashion subscription box is not just a purchase - it's an encounter with a story, a brand, and an ethos. Craft it with care, detail, and passion, and watch your subscription box business thrive.

Chapter 7. Building Your Brand: Creating a Name, Logo and Identity in a Crowded Market

Creating a unique and recognizable brand is essential in the competitive fashion industry. It's not enough to have a fantastic idea for a fashion subscription box; you need to communicate your brand's value proposition, personality, and ethos compellingly.

7.1. Understanding Your Brand

Before you can begin creating your brand name, logo, or identity, you must first understand your brand. Knowing your brand's purpose, values, and target audience forms the foundation of all brand-related decisions you make.

A solid brand has a clear purpose that goes beyond making money. Reflect on why you're creating this fashion subscription box. What are you hoping to change or improve upon in the fashion industry? What impact do you want to have on your customers' lives? Your brand's purpose can serve as an authentic point of connection with your potential customers, helping to set your brand apart.

Similarly vital are your brand's values. As a fashion brand, you may prioritize sustainable practices, body positivity, transparency, or diverse representations of beauty. Consumers today are thinking more about their purchases' societal and environmental impact, pushing brands to be more values-driven. By integrating your values into your brand from the very beginning, you can resonate more deeply with like-minded people.

Lastly, understand your target audience. Are you targeting fashion enthusiasts who want to keep up with the latest trends? Or perhaps you're targeting busy professionals who want to look stylish but don't have time to shop? Identifying your target audience lets you align your brand with their needs, preferences, and lifestyles, ensuring that your brand resonates with them.

7.2. Choosing a Brand Name

Choosing a brand name can be challenging, but it's crucial to get it right. Your brand name is the first impression potential customers have of your brand.

When brainstorming for your brand name, consider the following:

1. Relevance: The name should be relevant to the fashion industry and the specific type of fashion subscription box you're offering.

2. Uniqueness: It should be distinctively different from other fashion brands, especially those offering subscription boxes.

3. Memorable: The name should be catchy and easy to remember.

4. Positive Connotations: The name should evoke a positive emotional response or association.

5. Future Proof: It should be able to grow and evolve with your brand. Avoid names that could limit your business in future expansion and diversification.

6. Legal Availability: Make sure the name isn't already trademarked.

7.3. Designing a Logo

Once you have a strong brand name, the next step is to create a visually captivating logo that can largely influence how potential customers perceive your brand.

It's recommended to work with a professional designer. They can help translate your brand's essence into a visually appealing, recognizable, and unique logo. However, if you're starting on a shoestring budget, online platforms like Canva have easy-to-use logo design tools that require no design experience.

When designing your logo, keep the following in mind:

1. Simplicity: A simple logo design is easier to recognize and remember. It will also be more versatile, looking clear and distinguishable at any size and on various media.

2. Relevance: The logo should be relevant to the fashion industry and align with the style and tone of your brand; elegant and sophisticated, fun and playful, retro and quirky, and so on.

3. Versatility: Consider how your logo will look on different platforms, from your website and social media profiles to packaging and promotional materials. It should be design-friendly in both black and white and color.

4. Uniqueness: Avoid clichés and strive to create something original.

7.4. Creating a Brand Identity

Your brand identity is the visual manifestation of your brand, extending beyond just your name and logo. It includes your color palette, typography, imagery, packaging, website design, and social media aesthetics.

Establishing a cohesive and consistent brand identity helps build recognition and conveys professionalism. It also plays a significant role in communicating your brand's personality and differentiating your brand in the crowded fashion market.

Here are elements included in your brand identity:

1. Color Palette: Choose a color scheme that both represents your

brand and resonates with your target audience.

2. Typography: Your font choice should also match your brand's style, whether it be classic and elegant, bold and modern, or whimsical and playful.

3. Imagery: Use consistent, high-quality, and on-brand photos and illustrations across all platforms.

4. Packaging: Even your fashion subscription box's packaging is part of your brand identity—the unboxing experience should be memorable and spark excitement.

5. Website and Social Media: Consistency across all platforms, from colors and fonts to imagery and tone of voice, is crucial in creating a seamless brand experience.

Your brand is your fashion subscription box's heartbeat—it defines, differentiates, and drives your business. By understanding your brand, choosing a strong name, designing a compelling logo, and archiving cohesive brand identity, you can create a fashion subscription box brand that stands out in the crowded market and leaves lasting impressions.

Chapter 8. Marketing and Advertising 101: Spreading the Word and Attracting Subscribers

Understanding the intricate landscape of marketing and advertising is crucial to the success of your fashion subscription box business. To effectively put your brand on the map and attract the right audience, you must develop a robust marketing strategy, employ targeted advertising techniques, and imbibe the essence of relationship marketing.

8.1. Understanding Consumer Behavior

Your first step should be to understand the dynamics of consumer behavior. It gives you insights into how potential customers arrive at their purchasing decisions and how marketing stimuli influence their behavior. One of the key concepts in understanding consumer behavior is the marketing mix, also known as the 4Ps. They are: product (your fashion subscription box), price, place, and promotion.

To understand consumer behavior, you must identify and study your target market's demographics, psychographics, and purchase habits. This knowledge is instrumental in developing a marketing strategy tailored to your potential customers' needs and preferences.

8.2. Creating a Marketing Strategy

With key insights on consumer behavior, you can now create a successful marketing strategy. There are two overarching models to consider: inbound and outbound marketing.

Inbound marketing involves 'pulling' customers towards your products or services through content marketing, social media marketing, SEO, and branding. It is more interaction-focused, having the aim to provide value to the consumer.

On the other hand, outbound marketing is more traditional and involves 'pushing' products towards customers via direct emails, television and radio advertisements, billboards, etc.

A good marketing strategy should blend in both these models, and judiciously leverage digital and traditional marketing channels to reach out to potential consumers.

8.3. Branding

Branding is all about creating a unique identity for your business. Essential elements of branding include a catchy name, visually attractive logo, compelling tagline, and a distinctive visual theme that resonates with your target audience. A good branding strategy helps differentiate your fashion subscription box from competitors and creates a lasting impression in the minds of consumers.

8.4. Advertising

Advertising amplifies your marketing messages to a wider audience. In the dawn of digital marketing, various advertising channels like social media, search engines, email newsletters, and influencer marketing can be effectively employed. Identify the platforms your target market frequents and use them to distribute your advertisements.

Testing several advertising mediums allows you to gain insights into what resonates best with your audience, helping you refine your strategies accordingly.

8.5. SEO and Content Marketing

Search Engine Optimization (SEO) is about improving the visibility of your website on search engines. The higher the visibility, the more traffic you attract.

Content marketing, a subset of SEO, involves creating and distributing valuable, relevant, and consistent content to attract and retain a clearly defined audience. The key here is to publish a mix of informative blog articles, videos, infographics, and more that potential subscribers would find useful or entertaining.

8.6. Social Media Marketing

In today's interconnected world, social media marketing is a powerful tool for brands. It offers an opportunity to directly engage with your target audience and create a community around your fashion subscription box.

Platforms like Instagram are ideal for a fashion-forward business due to their visually driven nature. Use these platforms to share eye-catching images, engaging videos, behind-the-scenes footage, and stories of your subscription boxes.

8.7. Influencer Marketing

Influencer marketing can also be a powerful tool for your fashion subscription box business. Team up with fashion influencers whose style aligns with your brand. Their seal of approval can drive significant traffic and potential subscribers your way.

8.8. Relationship Marketing

Finally, relationship marketing is about building enduring relationships with your customers. It shifts the focus from individual sales to the entire customer lifecycle.

Remember, it's not enough to acquire subscribers, you must strive to retain them too. To successfully do this, encourage feedback, offer excellent customer service, and implement a loyalty program.

A strong marketing and advertising plan, teamed with your understanding of your customers, a sound business strategy, and your passion for fashion, will be your ticket to establishing, nurturing, and growing your own fashion subscription box empire. The next steps are up to you. Bring on the style, and watch your business soar!

Chapter 9. Customer Connection: Crafting a Personal and Positive User Experience

Crafting a personal and positive user experience is key to the success of your fashion subscription box business. Understanding your customers' needs, preferences, and expectations can elevate your brand and help you build lasting customer relationships.

9.1. Understanding Subscriber Personas

The first step in crafting a personalized customer experience is the creation of subscriber personas. Subscriber personas are fictional, generalized representations of your ideal customers to help you understand their fashion needs and purchasing behaviors. They can be based on a detailed analysis of your target market, as well as customer interviews and surveys.

To create a subscriber persona, consider the following factors:

- Age
- Gender
- Occupation
- Income level
- Fashion preferences
- Shopping habits

By understanding your customers in this manner, you can tailor your subscription boxes to match their preferences, ensuring satisfaction and long-term engagement.

9.2. Curating a Personalized Style Profile

Offering personalized subscription boxes is an effective way to cater to the differing fashion tastes and needs of your customers. Each subscriber should be asked to fill out a comprehensive style profile that includes their clothing sizes, preferred colors, styles, and patterns, any pieces they specifically need or want, their comfort zones, and any fashion risks they'd be open to.

The style profile ensures each subscriber receives a box tailored to their personal taste and lifestyle. A well-curated box increases the likelihood of repeat subscriptions, glowing reviews, and personal recommendations.

9.3. Enhancing the Unboxing Experience

An important part of the fashion subscription box business is the unboxing experience. It must be enjoyable and create anticipation for the next box. This can be achieved by packaging the items in an aesthetically pleasing manner. Consider branded boxes, colored tissue paper, ribbons, or stickers.

Including a personalized note or style guide can also enhance the unboxing experience. This makes your subscribers feel special and can help them understand how to style the contents of their box.

9.4. Building a Feedback Loop

Implementing a robust feedback loop allows you to understand your subscribers' views on their boxes. This can be done by regular email surveys or a feedback form on your website. Acknowledge their responses and make visible improvements based on their input.

9.5. Ensuring Efficient Customer Service

An efficient and empathetic customer service is crucial for any successful subscription box business. Train your customer support team to handle all types of inquiries effectively and ensure they have extensive knowledge about your products to accurately answer all customer questions.

9.6. Retaining Customers

To retain customers and encourage repeat subscriptions, always aim to exceed expectations with every box. Include surprise treats, exclusive discounts, or bonus items. Incentivizing referrals can help you acquire new customers while encouraging repeated subscriptions.

Remember, in the world of subscription boxes, happy customers are not just loyal, but are also the best advocates for your brand. Crafting a personal and positive user experience is an ongoing process that keeps your service exciting and desirable. If you consistently meet and exceed customer expectations, you are sure to make your mark in the competitive world of fashion subscription boxes.

Chapter 10. Logistics and Fulfillment: Ensuring Smooth Operations

Starting a fashion subscription box business is an exciting venture, and the keys to success are planning, attention to detail, and impeccable execution. Particularly, the Logistics and Fulfillment stage is crucial. Here's how to ensure smooth operations and keep your customers delighted.

10.1. Choosing Your Fulfillment Center

A fulfillment center is an essential piece of your logistics puzzle. These facilities store your products, pick and pack orders, and ship them to your customers. Selecting the right one means considering their expertise, cost, location, and scalability.

When choosing a facility, consider its proximity to your major customer bases. Closer locations mean reduced shipping cost and time.

Also consider the cost of fulfillment services. These services usually charge for receiving, storage, picking and packing, and shipping. Some may have additional charges like account setup or fee per order. Always ask for a detailed breakdown of costs.

Lastly, check if they can scale to meet higher demands during peak seasons or as your business grows.

10.2. Inventory Management

Accurate inventory management is indispensable. It ensures you have enough stock to meet demands without tying up resources in excess inventory.

Start by creating an inventory management plan. You should regularly check and update your inventory levels, both physical and on your management system. Set a re-order point to know when it's time to replenish stock.

You might also consider inventory management software. They can automate much of the tracking and reporting, saving you valuable time.

10.3. Packaging Your Boxes

The packaging of your subscription box is as important as what's inside. It protects your merchandise and provides the first impression of your brand to the customer.

Consider the size and weight of the items you plan on including in your boxes. This will determine the size and strength of the boxes you need.

The external look of the box is also important. Use it to project your brand and create a memorable unboxing experience. From the color of the box, to the design, wrapping paper, stickers, and personalized note, every detail should speak your brand.

10.4. Shipping & Delivery

Creating a positive shipping and delivery experience is an integral part of customer retention.

Firstly, choose a reliable shipping service that offers tracking options and insurance for lost packages. Also consider the shipping speed, cost, and the regions they cover.

Additionally, make sure your delivery times are clearly communicated to your customers. Be transparent about any delays and keep your customers updated about their delivery status.

10.5. Returns & Exchanges

No matter how well you operate, there will be returns and exchanges. It's important to have a well-defined policy for this. Your policy should guide how customers can process returns, who covers shipping costs, acceptable return conditions, and timeline for refunds or exchanges.

Your return process should be as hassle-free as possible. A smooth return process can turn a negative customer experience into a positive one, increasing the likelihood they will remain loyal to your brand.

10.6. Automating Processes

As your business grows, so will the complexity of your logistics operations. You should consider automating some tasks to enhance efficiency and reduce mistakes.

Automation can range from inventory management and order tracking to customer notifications and shipping label generation. Employing an Order Management System can streamline your operations, and free up your time to focus on other aspects of your business.

Each one of these sub-chapters outlines the fundamental components of Logistic and Fulfillment strategies for your fashion subscription box business. Following them ensures smoother operations, minimized chaos, and maximized customer satisfaction. From careful selection of your fulfilment center to effective inventory management, appealing packaging, efficient shipping & delivery, prudent return & exchange policies, and introducing automation, each is critical to your overall success. Now that you're armed with this detailed blueprint, you're well-prepared to navigate and thrive amidst the complexities of this engaging business model.

Chapter 11. Growing Your Business: Strategies for Expansion and Longevity

Understanding the dynamics of growing your business is critical, as your business will not thrive without a well-planned strategy for expansion and longevity. The factors mentioned below can help you to strategically expand and make sure your fashion subscription box business stays relevant for a long time.

11.1. Market Research

Re-evaluate the industry landscape and consumer behavior regularly. Studying changing fashion trends, understanding what your competitors are offering, an eye for the new big thing in fashion, and shifts in consumer preferences are all essential aspects of market research. Trends in sustainable fashion, wearable technology, and personalized clothing are gaining momentum and could provide a bridge to capturing a new set of customers.

11.2. Client Retention

A major building block to scaling and expanding your business is not just about acquiring new customers but retaining existing ones. Regularly updating the styles in your box, offering customization based on customer preferences, regular communication, and offering an excellent customer experience can ensure loyal subscribers. At the same time, rewarding customer loyalty can earn goodwill and positive word-of-mouth publicity.

11.3. Expanding Your Offerings

To stay ahead in the competitive fashion industry, you need to continually innovate and diversify. You can include new categories of clothing, accessories, jewelry, and even beauty products. Collaborating with brands and designers to offer exclusive items in your box can also be beneficial to your business.

11.4. Brand Partnerships

Forming strategic alliances and partnerships with different brands can provide mutual benefits. This not only allows both businesses to leverage each other's resources and customer base but also helps to increase brand visibility and reach.

11.5. Social Media Visibility

In the age of digital marketing, a strong online presence can drive significant growth in your customer base. Collaborating with influencers, running ad campaigns, showcasing success stories and the latest offerings, and making the most of digital marketing tools can help in amplifying your brand presence.

Your business's expansion and longevity do not solely rely on your products but also depend on the community you create around it. Therefore, fostering a strong, fashionable, and connected community will also help your business thrive.

11.6. Finance and Investment

Ensure you've got your finances in check. Consider expanding your budget for marketing, investing in website upgrades, user experience, and new technology as these can yield high returns in the long run. Also, don't shy away from seeking external funding or investors when needed. It's essential to have a robust financial strategy that supports your business's growth plans.

11.7. Scaling Production

As your business expands, your production and supply chain should keep up. Having a scalable business model, good relationships with suppliers, efficient inventory management, and well-planned logistics will help smoothly run your operations as the demand for your products increases.

11.8. Legal Considerations

Understanding legal obligations such as patents, copyrights, trademarking, licensing of brands and designs are necessary to avoid possible future complications. Hence, ensure you have an excellent legal body that guides you through these processes.

11.9. Sustainable Practices

Incorporating sustainable practices into your business has numerous benefits. Customers are becoming increasingly aware of the impact of their purchases on the environment, so adding eco-friendly options to your boxes could enhance your brand's value and demonstrate social responsibility.

11.10. International Expansion

After achieving a certain level of success domestically, you might consider international expansion. Research thoroughly before venturing into a new geographical market. Understand their customs, consumer behavior, and be careful with cultural sensitivity in fashion.

Growing a business takes time, effort, and patience; but with a plan and strategy in place, you can see your fashion subscription box business expand and thrive in the long-run.